Heaven Is
For Real

One Man's Amazing Journey To Heaven

Dr Michael H Yeager

Endorsements:

I feel honored to endorse a book that is being used to minister to the church and to lost souls. This new book of Mike Yeager's will change your life.

Not only does Mike passionately give his readers the intimate details of his journey but also gives insightful Scriptures for anyone to receive Jesus as their Savior. I know this book will inspire you to arise from complacency to reach out to a lost world. His book is a catalyst for conquering defeat. Joanna Coe Herndon

Mike Yeager's testimony unveils the realities of heaven. This book will stir in you a passion for souls as Mike clearly explains the eternal destiny of those who know Christ. This book is destined to awaken a generation to the realities of heaven and the afterlife. Gary Bailey

We have known Michael Yeager for over forty years and find him to be a man of integrity, honor, and trust. He is full of God's love and God's Word which have helped him weather storms that have made him a general in the army of God. He has God's heart for souls and God's love for the kingdom and the King. We are blessed to know him, and we recommend him and his work to all who are interested in growing in building God's kingdom on earth as it is in heaven. His apostolic call is evident to us in his unlimited vision and the establishment of ongoing works in this land and others. Al and Billie Deck

ISBN:1533422575
ISBN-13:9781533422576

DEDICATION

I dedicate this book to all those who are hungry and thirsty after righteousness; who yearn and long for a harvest of souls, who are waiting for the early and latter rain, and the great and final outpouring of the Holy Ghost. I dedicate this book to all of those who will embrace the fear of the Lord (which is the beginning of wisdom), and at the same time revel In God's love. To those who cry out to be partakers of the heart of the Father, the Son, and the Holy Ghost, whose very heart yearns for the salvation of the multitudes. Oh precious Lord, pour out your Spirit once again upon humanity as in the days of old. May your glorious bride rise up with sickles in their hands, and divine love in their hearts for the lost. The harvest is great, but the laborers are few.

Heaven Is For Real

CONTENTS

ACKNOWLEDGMENTS

*To our heavenly Father and His wonderful love.

*To our Lord, Savior and Master —Jesus Christ, who saved us and set us free because of His great love for us.

*To the Holy Spirit, who leads and guides us into the realm of miraculous living every day.

*To all of those who had a part in helping us get this book ready for the publishers.

*To my Wife Kathleen and our precious children, Michael, Daniel, Steven, Stephanie, Catherine Yu, who is our precious daughter-in-law, and Naomi, who is now with the Lord!

Preface: You Better Not Lie!

One day I picked up a book by a well-known author. This book had come highly recommended to me by one of my favorite preachers. The topic was about supernatural visitations. This was something I was interested in, because of my experience with having been taken into heaven.

As I began to read this book, there were experiences he said he had, which did not seem to line up with the Scriptures. I did not want to judge his heart, but we do have the responsibility to examine everything in the light of God's Word. As I was pondering upon the stories of this book, the Spirit of the Lord spoke to my heart. It was as if He was standing right there next to me, speaking audibly. What He spoke to me was rather shocking! God told me that the writer of this book would be dead in three months from a heart attack. I asked the Lord why He was telling me this. He said because the stories in the man's book were exaggerated, that judgment was coming. The Lord warned me that day that if I were ever to do the same thing, judgment would come to me.

When the Spirit of the Lord spoke this to me, I turned and told my wife. I held the book up and said, in a very quiet whispering wavering voice, "Honey, the man who wrote this book will be dead in three months from a heart attack." Plus, I told her why the Lord told me this. I wish I had been wrong. However, three months later, the man died from a heart attack. The issue here is not the minister who died from a heart attack. The issue is the warning that God had spoken to me personally about judgment, if I exaggerated. That's why I'm striving to not exaggerate the retelling of the stories within this book about me, my wife, and my family's lives.

CHAPTER ONE
A Divine Appointment

Dear reader, before I can take you on this journey I need to clarify a number of issues and facts that might help you understand what happened to me and why it happened. I do not believe that you have picked this book up by mistake or accident. But rather, this is a divine appointment, the providence of God, which has brought us together. What I am about to share with you are four supernatural encounters which the Lord has allowed me to experience. The first was an experience that I had as a child. The second experience is about when an angel took me to heaven. The third is when by a dream where God took me into the center of creation. The fourth is an amazing dream that was very precise and prophetic that God gave me in 2014. I believe that all of these encounters were explicitly given for the reaping of the harvest. Please understand that God's greatest desire is that souls might be converted. All He has done has been for the salvation of sinners. He came to seek and save the lost.

"For the Son of man is come to save that which was lost" (Matt. 18:11).

"I will seek that which was lost, and bring again that which was driven away, and will bind up that which was broken, and will strengthen that which was sick" (Ezek. 34:16).

My journey to heaven took place in the spring of 1975. You might have the false assumption that an experience that transpired over 40 years ago might not have an impact upon my life still. But actually it's the opposite. To this very day, even as I recount this occurrence, it shakes and grips me to the very core of my being. As I reflect upon what the Lord allowed me to experience it is as if it was just yesterday. I do not know how to fully express how amazing and mind-boggling this journey was. Though it lasted only hours in the physical world, in the spirit realm it seemed as if I was there for an eternity.

"For a thousand years in thy sight are but as yesterday when it is past, and as a watch in the night" (Ps. 90:4).

"But, beloved, be not ignorant of this one thing, that one day is with the Lord as a thousand years, and a thousand years as one day"(2 Pet. 3:8).

You might think that what I'm about to share with you is extremely exaggerated, but I can tell you without a shadow of a doubt that I am not embellishing in the least my journey to Heaven . If anything, I find myself at a loss to fully express what Heaven is really like. I cannot speak for others, but for me it was more real than the flesh and blood world I live in. The Apostle Paul shares with us that he himself experienced this to some extent.

"I knew a man in Christ above fourteen years ago (whether in the body, I cannot tell; or whether out of the body, I cannot tell: God knoweth;) such an one caught up to the third heaven. And I knew such a man, (whether in the body, or out of the body, I cannot tell: God knoweth;)" (2 Cor. 12:2-3).

To me, my experience was both physical and literal. It was not a vision or a dream. I could touch, taste, see, smell, and hear all that transpired. My five senses and my emotional, mental, and psychological perceptions were even more alive in the encounter than they are now. It was as if they were supernaturally enhanced and amplified by God in order for me to experience all of the amazing realities of eternity, dwelling and living in the presence of God.

Psalm 16:11 Thou wilt shew me the path of life: in thy presence is fulness of joy; at thy right hand there are pleasures for evermore.

Revelation 7:15 Therefore are they before the throne of God, and serve him day and night in his temple: and he that sitteth on the throne shall dwell among them.16 They shall hunger no more, neither thirst any more; neither shall the sun light on them, nor any heat.17 For the Lamb which is in the midst of the throne shall feed them, and shall lead them unto living fountains of waters: and God shall wipe away all tears from their eyes.

Revelation 22:5 And there shall be no night there; and they need no candle, neither light of the sun; for the Lord God giveth them light: and they shall reign for ever and ever.

Divine Encounters

The church of the twenty-first century has lost the understanding that we absolutely need supernatural encounters with the presence of the Lord. From Genesis to Revelation we see encounter after encounter of men and women with the divine supernatural. It is by supernatural visitations and visions that God reveals Himself and His will for humanity. It is also by these divine visitations that He transforms, molds, and shapes His people for a specific task, even as the potter does the clay. The revelation that we have of the Word of God was by divine encounter.

"For the prophecy came not in old time by the will of man: but holy men of God spake as they were moved by the Holy Ghost" (2 Pet. 1:21).

"The Spirit of the LORD spake by me, and his word was in my tongue" (2 Sam. 23:2).

If we were to eliminate every supernatural encounter in the Bible, I dare say there would not be a Bible. If you look at the men and women of God throughout history, those used in any significant way had experienced visions, visitations, translations, and angelic encounters. We could begin with Enoch, Abraham, Jacob, Joseph, Moses, Joshua and Caleb, the judges and continue all the way down through history to the end of the New Testament.

I believe that God wants every one of His people to have a supernatural biblical experience. As you read my journal—this book—you'll discover that if I had not had a divine encounter thirty-five years ago, I may have never been saved and rescued from the powers of darkness. I would have been lost and suffering with those who are in the flames of hell forever. Am I telling you to seek a divine encounter? No; I am saying that as you draw near to God that the veil between the flesh and the Spirit will at times disappear. You will find yourself stepping into the mind-boggling realm of the Spirit. Read Revelation chapter 1 when John was in the Spirit on the Lord's day:

"And I turned to see the voice that spake with me. And being turned, I saw seven golden candlesticks; And in the midst of the seven candlesticks one like unto the Son of man, clothed with a garment down to the foot, and girt about the paps with a golden girdle. His head and his hairs were white like wool, as white as snow; and his eyes were as a flame of fire; And his feet like unto fine brass, as if they burned in a furnace; and his voice as the sound of many waters. And he had in his right hand seven stars: and out of his mouth went a sharp two-edged sword: and his countenance was as the sun shineth in his strength. And when I saw him, I fell at his feet as dead. And he laid his right hand upon me, saying unto me, Fear not; I am the first and the last: I am he that liveth, and was dead; and, behold, I am alive for evermore, Amen; and have the keys of hell and of death" (Rev. 1:12-18).

The experience I had of going to heaven is not as unusual as some would think it might be. If you read the journals of former revivalists you will discover that in the Welsh revival, John Wesley's revivals, George Whitfield's, Charles Finney's, and many others, masses of people fell to the ground and went into a trance (like a coma) and experienced visions of heaven and hell. It is the Spirit of the Lord that comes upon His people and sinners to reveal divine truths and revelations.

"It is the spirit that quickeneth; the flesh profiteth nothing" (John 6:63).

"Then he answered and spake unto me, saying, This is the word of the LORD unto Zerubbabel, saying, Not by might, nor by power, but by my Spirit, saith the LORD of hosts" (Zech. 4:6).

Let me also add that Scripture says we have not because we ask not. I believe by the Spirit of God, that we need to begin to ask and believe God to give us certain experiences. (We are not seeking these experiences.) These are not experiences that we will consume upon our lust, but these are desires that God would put in our hearts in order to fulfill His divine will in the earth. Whatever we ask of God we must make sure that we believe in our hearts that it is His will and that it is scripturally and biblically correct.

"Or what man is there of you, whom if his son ask bread, will he give him a stone? Or if he ask a fish, will he give him a serpent? If ye then, being evil, know how to give good gifts unto your children, how much more shall your Father which is in heaven give good things to them that ask him?" (Matt. 7:9-11).

I cannot emphasize enough the importance of moving in the power of the Holy Spirit! God never intended us to reap the harvest without the power of His Spirit.

"For as the body without the spirit is dead, so faith without works is dead also" (James 2:26).

"And, being assembled together with them, commanded them that they should not depart from Jerusalem, but wait for the promise of the Father, which, saith he, ye have heard of me" (Acts 1:4).

If we really want to see God move in our lives, families, and churches we need to completely die to all symbolism, traditions, and trappings that would hinder or grieve the Holy Ghost.

"O foolish Galatians, who hath bewitched you, that ye should not obey the truth, before whose eyes Jesus Christ hath been evidently set forth, crucified among you? This only would I learn of you, Received ye the Spirit by the works of the law, or by the hearing of faith? Are ye so foolish? having begun in the Spirit, are ye now made perfect by the flesh? Have ye suffered so many things in vain? if it be yet in vain. He therefore that ministereth to you the Spirit, and worketh miracles among you, doeth he it by the works of the law, or by the hearing of faith?" (Gal. 3:1-5).

Was My Experiences Biblical?

"For the word of God is quick, and powerful, and sharper than any two-edged sword, piercing even to the dividing asunder of soul and spirit, and of the joints and marrow, and is a discerner of the thoughts and intents of the heart" (Heb. 4:12).

My journey to heaven took place even before I knew what the Bible had to say on the subject. If any of these experiences or any of the other experiences I have had through the years had been contrary to the teachings of Christ or the prophets, I would adamantly reject them, turn my back on them, and declare that they were not of God. A God-given vision of heaven or hell or any other visitation would never contradict Scriptures. I am not sharing with you something I made up out of the figment of my own imagination for the purpose of selling books or to make a name for myself. What you are about to read truly happened to me. Please understand that when God gives visions, dreams, and divine encounters that many of these experiences could be revealed by shadows and illustrations of spiritual truths that He wants us to grasp and understand.

"But the fearful, and unbelieving, and the abominable, and murderers, and whoremongers, and sorcerers, and idolaters, and all liars, shall have their part in the lake which burneth with fire and brimstone: which is the second death" (Rev. 21:8).

Something Is About to Happen

In regards to my journey to heaven, it was similar to my journey to hell in that it did not seem to me to be a vision or a dream. But it was a physical event that was amplified, I'll even say

7

multiplied, beyond that of the normal five senses. I will not be able to share with you all that transpired on this particular journey because the Spirit of God spoke to me things that are not lawful to speak on this side of heaven. But just to give you a "heads up," what God showed me was to take place upon the earth in my lifetime has not yet happened. But I have been sensing with great anticipation in my heart that those hidden events are about to explode upon the pages of human history.

We are about to see things that no other previous generation has seen. For the body of Christ, the church, these events will be amazing, marvelous, wonderful, and yet terrifying. But to those of the world who do not know Christ, it will be like a never-ending horror story and nightmare. We have truly come to the end of the ages.

Not too long ago a young child came to me and told me that he had what he thought was a vision. He described to me an hourglass. He did not know what an hourglass was. But in the very top of the hourglass there was only a very small amount of sand left. I truly believe with all my heart that time is running out. And that what we do for God, and the kingdom, we needed to do quickly.

Where I am about to take you will not tickle or please your flesh. It will not make you want to shout, sing all, or dance. But I believe it'll make you weep and wail for the lost, the damned, and the dying. Why? In order that revival might break forth across the nations. For the Lord of the harvest is patient until He receives the early in latter rain.

"Say not ye, There are yet four months, and then cometh harvest? behold, I say unto you, Lift up your eyes, and look on the fields; for they are white already to harvest" (John 4:35

CHAPTER TWO
My Life Story

In order to help you to comprehend what you are about to read, I need to give you a quick synopsis of my life. I believe that for all of us God has a divine destiny and purpose, a heavenly plan. I believe that from the moment we are conceived in our mother's womb, the Holy Spirit begins to work in us to bring about the Heavenly Father's perfect will. At the same time, the enemy of our souls and the demonic world is doing all it can to keep us from the revelation of God's purpose for our lives. And if at all possible, it is trying to drag us to hell.

"The thief cometh not, but for to steal, and to kill, and to destroy: I am come that they might have life, and that they might have it more abundantly" (John 10:10).

As human beings we are literally suspended between heaven and hell in a spiritual sense. Every choice we make brings us either closer to hell or to heaven. Our final destiny is really in our own hands. Many have erroneously misunderstood the doctrine of predestination.

"Who will have all men to be saved, and to come unto the knowledge of the truth"(1 Tim. 2:4).

"The Lord is not slack concerning his promise, as some men count slackness; but is longsuffering to us-ward, not willing that any should perish, but that all should come to repentance"(2 Pet. 3:9).

The Scriptures cannot be understood with the carnal mind or natural reasoning. What is amazing is that even in our wayward, sinful, and rebellious condition, God moves upon our hearts and lives.

You see, my mother gave birth to me three months early. I was a premature baby with physical disabilities. My lungs were underdeveloped which caused me difficulty in breathing. I remember as a little boy many times looking out through an oxygen tent in a local hospital. My feet also were turned inward, so doctors had to place my feet in braces for approximately five months. My older brother and sister had similar problems with their feet.

The inner bones of my ears were not developed correctly. They were "frozen" in place, and when I became congested, they would not allow the fluids to drain into my sinuses. This created tremendous buildup of pressure, which punctured my ear drums, causing a hearing disability.

My tongue was attached to the bottom part of my mouth. I went through numerous operations in order to give me use of it in speech. I was never able to speak fluently even though I went to speech therapy classes. To this day all I can remember of my speech teacher is that she had very large lips. To a great extent most people could not understand a lot of what I was saying. What was most embarrassing is that I could not even say my last name correctly (Yeager). Instead of saying "car," I could only say "cow." Instead of "rat," I would say "wat." Instead of saying "tree," I would say "twee." My tongue simply would not cooperate and flex the way it was meant to. I thank

God that after I gave my heart to Jesus Christ and was filled with the Holy Ghost, speaking in tongues, all of these infirmities were healed, including my speech impediment.

Because of these disabilities and to a great extent my very dysfunctional family, I began to get in trouble at an early age. I remember the first time I became intoxicated with alcohol. I was at a cousin's wedding. I was only about seven years old when I became extremely drunk and sick. By the time I was eighteen, I was an alcoholic. This seemed to be a generational curse. Thank God this has been broken over our whole family.

At fifteen years of age I quit school and began to run with a gang. Those in this gang where all older than myself. Our stomping grounds were located right outside of Chicago, between Chicago and Waterford, Wisconsin. We were involved in drugs, stealing, violence, alcohol, and other forms of immorality and wickedness that I will not mention. This led to a life of fear and hate, rebellion, and lawlessness. I had an overwhelming anger expressly for myself. The law finally caught up to me at the age of sixteen, and I was given a choice to either join the military or face prosecution.

I passed my GED (General Education Degree), and I chose to join the Navy. When I first applied, I was turned down because of my hearing disabilities. But our family doctor convinced them that no further harm could happen to my hearing. But because of the immovable bones in my ears, the first time I flew in a high altitude jet my left eardrum burst. I had to be taken to a hospital to have that eardrum replaced.

After I completed boot camp at the Great Lakes Naval base in Illinois, I continued my education in the same location to be an electrician's mate. I graduated at the bottom of my class. My grades were so low that I did not even receive my stripes for E4, which was standard.

Then I was shipped to San Diego, California, for training in the use and the repair of sixteen millimeter projectors. From there I was sent to Adak, Alaska, an island in the Aleutian Island Chain thirteen hundred miles southwest of Anchorage. In the Navy it is considered what is called "sea duty" because of its desolate and remote location. While on Adak my downward spiral continued with an ever-increasing alcohol and drug problem. I began to sell drugs (basically, blonde hashish) in order to support my habit. Then on my nineteenth birthday, February 18, 1975, I had finally come to the end of my road. I was sick of my existence. I hated myself with all of my shortcomings and all of my failures.

In my opinion my whole life was nothing but one, big fat zero. All I could see was the foolishness of my life, the vanity of my existence. I did not want to live another day, not another hour, or even another minute. At this time in my life I did not realize that there were demonic powers which were out to destroy me and drag my soul to hell.

Suicide

The only way of escape that I could see was for me to kill myself. My older brother (by four years) had tried to commit suicide when he was about eighteen years old by taking an overdose of medicine. I remember finding him on the floor of our living room looking as if he was already dead. I called for an ambulance, and thank God, they arrived in time to pump his stomach. It was not even a year later when I found my older sister (by two years) in the same condition. Thank God, once again they arrived in time to save my sister. I had determined in my heart that I was not going to make the same mistake that my brother and sister had made.

Prior to this I had gone to a local hard ware and hunting store and purchased a very sharp, large survival knife. The thought entered my mind that with this knife I could escape my useless and horrible life. I waited until there was no one left in our barracks. I went into what we call "the head" in the Navy, which is another word for the bathroom. I put that knife to my wrist with every intent and purpose of slitting my wrist, cutting down through my arteries, and ending my miserable life.

I remember weeping uncontrollably, feeling sorry for myself. But as I began to apply pressure to the knife against my wrist, all of a sudden something mysterious and supernatural happened. It was as if an invisible blanket came floating down through the ceiling of that little bathroom, floating down on top of me. I could feel it. To me it was very real, physical, and tangible. In one single moment an overwhelming, heart-stopping, mind-boggling fear hit me like a ton of bricks. It was what I now know as the fear of the Lord. I had never known the fear of the Lord before this experience. But at that very moment by the Spirit of God I knew that I knew, that I was going to hell. I knew that I deserved hell; I knew that I belonged in hell. I knew that I had sinned against a holy and righteous God. Hell was reaching out for me. I knew that hell had a right to claim me. At that moment I did not know why I knew this, but I knew it. I remember beginning to shake so violently under this conviction—this reality—that I dropped my knife into the sink.

"The fear of the LORD is the beginning of wisdom" (Prov. 9:10).

"My flesh trembleth for fear of thee; and I am afraid of thy judgments" (Ps. 119:120).

The Scriptures declare that at the end of the age the fear of the Lord would depart from the earth. A number of years ago as I was preparing for a Sunday morning service (I have been a pastor now for over thirty years), the Spirit of the Lord spoke to me. He asked me what I thought was a very simple question. He said to me, *"Son, why did Lucifer fall?"* I thought for a moment and replied, "Lord, because he wanted to be God." This answer is biblically correct, but I discovered that there is more to it than just that.

"How art thou fallen from heaven, O Lucifer, son of the morning! how art thou cut down to the ground, which didst weaken the nations! For thou hast said in thine heart, I will ascend into heaven, I will exalt my throne above the stars of God: I will sit also upon the mount of the congregation, in the sides of the north: I will ascend above the heights of the clouds; I will be like the most High. Yet thou shalt be brought down to hell, to the sides of the pit"(Is. 14:12-15).

Once again the Spirit of God asked me the same question, "Why did Lucifer fall?" Again I answered the same. The Lord asked me a third time, "Son, why did Lucifer fall?" I finally answered with, "Lord, I don't know. Would You please tell me why he fell?" The Lord spoke to me and said, "Because none of the angelic realm, the spiritual realm, or creation itself had ever seen My wrath, My anger, or vengeance. All they had ever known was My goodness and love." Satan and his followers did not maintain the fear of the Lord in their hearts. The Lord told me that this present generation is making the exact same terrible mistake! He said, "They do not understand that I am a consuming fire." This is one reason that the church is rampant with sin and disobedience to God and His holy Word. God is a holy and righteous God. He cannot allow sin to continue.

"For our God is a consuming fire" (Heb. 12:29).

"Follow peace with all men, and holiness, without which no man shall see the Lord" (Heb. 12:14).

Throughout eternity not only will the saints walk in the love of Christ, but they will forever have built within them the fear of the Lord. The fear of the Lord is not a curse. It is a divine gift from the heavenly Father. It is placed within the heart of the saint in order to keep him within the will of God to protect him from the lies and deceptions of that which is evil.

"And they shall be my people, and I will be their God: And I will give them one heart, and one way, that they may fear me forever, for the good of them, and of their children after them: And I will make an everlasting covenant with them, that I will not turn away from them, to do them good; but I will put my fear in their hearts, that they shall not depart from me. Yea, I will rejoice over them to do them good, and I will plant them in this land assuredly with my whole heart and with my whole soul"(Jer. 32:38-41).

My First Experience as a Child

There was only one other time I could remember having experienced a supernatural visitation. I was about six years old. Even during those years, I had caused my parents all kinds of heartache and sorrow. I was always getting into trouble, yelling, screaming, cursing, and disobeying. I caused my mother, Shirley, so much heartache that once, in utter frustration, she told me that I had to be the devil himself. She never knew how those words deeply affected me. No matter how hard I tried to be good, I just got worse. I remember as a little boy I would get up on the sink in our little bathroom, look in the mirror, and run my hands through my hair. I was absolutely positive that I could feel two large lumps beginning to form on my skull. I was almost positive that I was the devil himself.

One night during this time I had gotten up to go to the bathroom. It was a cold winter night, and there was at least a foot of snow on the ground. The house was very quiet because everyone else in my family was sleeping. The light of the moon was shining through the bathroom window. The window was made of milk-colored, perforated glass. As I looked through it, a shiver ran from my head to my feet. There in the milk-colored glass I saw three crosses. The middle one seemed to be three-dimensional. An overwhelming sense of love radiated from the middle cross. Then as I looked at it very intently, I thought there was a figure of a man hanging on it. I saw blood flowing from his hands and feet and his head. The next thing I knew, I was crying. I wept uncontrollably and did not understand what it was all about. Yet somehow I knew that God had touched me.

For the next two weeks, I was totally different, almost a saint. I believe it was because of this experience that I began to have the desire to be a Roman Catholic priest. My mother was completely amazed at the change that overtook me. I became very polite, kind, and helpful. No one had to ask me to help; I simply did it. And even when the other children mocked me, I just ignored them instead of fighting back. I even quit aggravating my sister, Debbie. But I'm sorry to say that this did not last very long. Before I knew it I became worse than I was before. This spiritual experience as a child, this encounter that I had with God, was forgotten as if it had never happened.

Now here I was, thirteen years later, experiencing another supernatural visitation while trying to kill myself. But this was much stronger. I turned my back on that sink, walked out of that little bathroom, and threw myself down on the floor next to my military bunk. The presence of God was so real I could barely breathe or move.

New Creation

As I cried out to Jesus, He supernaturally stepped into my life. It was as if a bolt of lightning hit me. Love, supernatural awesome love, began to roll over me, wave after wave after glorious wave. Instantly in my heart I knew without a shadow of a doubt that God loved me, died for me, rose from the dead, and was coming back for me. It was as if buckets of tangible love poured over the top of me and into me. I went from mind-boggling, overwhelming fear to an absolute, complete, and overwhelming love. Jesus set me free completely and instantly. I was free from the desire and need to do drugs! I was free from alcohol! I was free from ungodly desires! I was free from chewing tobacco and three packs of cigarettes a day! The overwhelming depression, self-pity, and self-loathing were gone. The emptiness that I had experienced and tried to fill with everything the world had to offer—alcohol and drugs, pornography and sex, fast cars and sports, materialism and money, violence and fighting—was now filled with an eternal quality, the presence of Christ in my heart.

"Therefore if any man be in Christ, he is a new creature: old things are passed away; behold, all things are become new" (2 Cor. 5:17).

I was so radically changed and transformed by the Spirit, by the power of God, that I fell in love with Christ head over heels. There is no way that I could ever do enough to express my love and devotion or the gratefulness that was in my heart for Jesus at that moment. For the first time in my life I knew what love was, or should I say who love is. It is the Father, the Son, and the Holy Ghost. And now because Jesus Christ lives in my heart it has created within me an amazing, overwhelming love for others. I received an overwhelming desire to go out and to tell others about Jesus Christ and what He had done for me.

"And hope maketh not ashamed; because the love of God is shed abroad in our hearts by the Holy Ghost which is given unto us" (Rom. 5:5).

Not only had He rescued me from an immoral life, from suicide, and from hell, but within a short period of time I was healed of all of my physical ailments and disabilities.

"Who his own self bare our sins in his own body on the tree, that we, being dead to sins, should live unto righteousness: by whose stripes ye were healed" (1 Pet. 2:24).

"That it might be fulfilled which was spoken by Esaias the prophet, saying, Himself took our infirmities, and bare our sicknesses" (Matt. 8:17).

Immediately I began to devour the Word of God, especially the four gospels, Matthew, Mark, Luke, and John. Daily I grew in my knowledge of God's awesome goodness and love and the wonderful plan He has for you and me. But within my heart I knew that there had to be a greater level of love and compassion and concern for the lost, the damned, the doomed, and the dying. There had to be a deeper level for those who were blind and ignorant of their spiritual condition even as I had been. So I began to cry out to God intensely, asking Him to allow me to have a supernatural experience of hell. I wanted this in order that I would have a greater and deeper compassion, a deeper love, a deeper understanding for the lost.

I truly wanted to know the pains, the sorrows, the torments, the fears, and the agonies of those in hell. I wanted to weep and wail, to travail in a broken heart over the unconverted in order to reach them more effectively. I did not realize at this time that it was the Holy Spirit who was putting this prayer in my mouth. Paul proclaimed:

"My little children, of whom I travail in birth again until Christ be formed in you" (Gal. 4:19).

"Be in pain, and labor to bring forth, O daughter of Zion, like a woman in travail" (Mic. 4:10a).

The Spirit of the Lord began to take me into deep and fervent intercessory prayer. He began to teach me how to stand in the gap on behalf of others, to walk the floor for hours on end for souls. He taught me how to lay upon my face in His presence until there was a breakthrough. He showed me how to submit my body as an instrument, a vessel He could pray through. Every believer, every child of God is called to intercede and travail for souls. It has been said that there is power in prayer. I know what people mean when they make that statement, but it's not exactly accurate. There are many religions in which people pray obsessively. But of course it brings no good results. The power does not come from the prayer, but the power comes from the One that we are crying out to! Jesus declared: Amazingly God did answer this prayer of wanting to experience the realities of hell. You can read this experience in my book: **Hell Is for Real.**

"I am the vine, ye are the branches: He that abideth in me, and I in him, the same bringeth forth much fruit: for with out me ye can do nothing" (John 15:5)

CHAPTER THREE
My Journey to Heaven

The description of my journey to heaven is much briefer than that which I experienced when the Lord sent me to hell. The reason for this is that there are many things the Lord spoke to my heart and revealed to me, things that are "not lawful" for me to share.

"How that he was caught up into paradise, and heard unspeakable words, which it is not lawful for a man to utter" (2 Cor. 12:4).

"And the vision of the evening and the morning which was told is true: wherefore shut thou up the vision; for it shall be for many days" (Dan. 8:26).

This divine, angelic visitation happened approximately one month after I had gone to hell. This time I was all alone praying and crying out to God in our dormitory. I had been walking around with my hands in the air praying, singing, and talking to the Lord. Suddenly, my room was filled with an overwhelming presence of the Lord. It was so real that I fell to my knees and tears began to flow freely from my eyes. I found myself lying flat upon my face totally caught up in this overwhelming presence. My face was buried into the floor. I was weeping, crying, and praying. All of a sudden the room I was in was filled with an intense bright light. I lifted my head to see what in the world was going on. There in front of me was a portal. It was like an opening into another world. It was not square like a regular door opening. This doorway was circular on the top like an archway. The light coming from this portal was so bright and brilliant that I could not really even look at it. This was not my imagination playing tricks on me. There literally was a brilliant, shining portal into another realm right there in my military dorm.

I was completely petrified and did not know what to do. It felt as if I was frozen to the floor and unable even to move a muscle. A holy fear gripped my whole body, my mind, and my five senses. I could see that someone was walking toward me through this tunnel of light. To my shock and amazement out of this glorious portal of light stepped a figure of a man. This was no ordinary man. He was about seven feet tall with a broad chest and shoulders with a slender waist. His flesh blazed like the burning of an arch welder, and he had dark hair. His face did not seem to have ever been shaved. In other words, there was no stubble on his face. He had the stature of a body builder only more solid and almost unearthly. He wore a glistening, brilliant, white gown with a slightly transparent belt around his waist that glowed of silver. I was not able to move or talk in his presence. When this angelic being finally spoke to me his voice seemed to fill the whole room. He said to me, ***"Fear not; for I have come from the presence of the Almighty to show you things that must come to pass."***

I remember asking him, "What is your name?" He replied, "My name is of no importance. I am but a messenger sent to you with a message and a mission that is greater than I." Inwardly, I wondered what kind of purpose could there be in this visitation. As I reflect upon this experience, I can tell you that parts of it are completely missing from my memory. It's not that it was not real or substantial, because it was just as real as the flesh and blood world that I find myself in right now. I believe the reason that parts of this visitation are missing is because it is sealed away in my heart, and I am not able or permitted to reveal or repeat all that transpired.

Revelation 10:4 And when the seven thunders had uttered their voices, I was about to write: and I heard a voice from heaven saying unto me, Seal up those things which the seven thunders uttered, and write them not.

This angel spoke to me and said, "Now you must come with me., For there are many things you must see." This angel stepped forward, leaned down, and took me by the right hand. He lifted me to my feet. The way he lifted me up I must have been as light as a feather to him. It was as if he rippled with unlimited strength, and I was like a little child in his hands. I knew in my heart that he could easily have kill me without any effort. This was my first experience in a tangible way with an angelic being. From that time up to now I have been protected, provided through and helped by these amazing messengers of God. For instance, I'm convinced an angelic being drove my car for many hours once when I was totally caught up praising and worshiping God as I drove down the road with my hands off the steering wheel.

Jesus Took the Wheel

In May of 1975 I was driving my sister's 1973 red Maverick from Canada to Wisconsin. I had been discharged from the Navy since I had completed my military service. My sister was in the Air Force and was stationed in New Mexico. She asked me to drive her car from New Mexico to Anchorage, Alaska, which was her next tour of duty. I agreed, since I had driven the Alcan Freeway during the onset of winter the previous year. From Anchorage to Seattle is 2,300 miles long. (At that time I was only eighteen years old and not yet saved. I cover that experience in another book.) I was planning to return to Alaska to go out and minister to the Yupik Indians, so I agreed to drive her vehicle all the way to Anchorage.

I experienced heavy rains as I headed up through Canada on the dirt road which took me to Fairbanks. To my disappointment, I had to stop and turn around because the bridges were all washed out. They didn't know when they would open the roads that were washed out due to flooding rivers. The thought occurred to me about driving her car back to Wisconsin where my parents lived.

Looking back, I realize that God was in this event. I came out of the mountains of Canada singing and worshipping God in the Spirit as the sun was at its peak in the sky above me. As I worshipped God, the car became filled with the tangible presence of the Lord. I was overwhelmed by His goodness and love. The reality of His love was so strong that I began to weep. The inside of my car was instantly filled with a light, glistening fog. I was so caught up in worshiping the Lord that I raised my hands toward heaven, taking them off the steering wheel. Time seemed to stand still as I was ushered into this incredible realm of mind-boggling worship.

Eventually my hands came back to the steering wheel as the fog was dissipating. I noticed the sun, which had been in the middle of the sky, was just now peeking over the horizon and it was beginning to get dark. At that time I did not check the mileage of the car , but I know my car had gone many miles without me steering it. Someone had driven my car as I was caught up in this intense RAM of worship!

"Bless the LORD, ye his angels, that excel in strength, that do his commandments, hearkening unto the voice of his word" (Ps. 103:20).

Back to My Visitation

I remember holding this angels hand with my right hand. There was tremendous heat coming from it. It was not the same type of heat I had experienced in hell. It is literally impossible to explain to you the sensations and feelings I was experiencing at that moment. The fire I felt in his hand was a holy fire. It seemed as if the heat was a living thing. Power radiated from his body. I cannot remember the color of his eyes. This angel was not Jesus. He was simply a messenger sent to take me into the heavens.

"Who maketh his angels spirits; his ministers a flaming fire" (Ps. 104:4).

"Are they not all ministering spirits, sent forth to minister for them who shall be heirs of salvation?" (Heb. 1:14).

Portal to Heaven

I found myself being led by this angel into the portal doorway of brilliant light. As I stepped into this light, this light flooded my whole being. All of the filthiness of the flesh felt as if it just melted right off of me. For the first time in my life I felt completely pure and holy. At that moment I was literally transformed—soul, mind, and body! My mind became extremely clear and more comprehensive than I had ever thought possible. A whole new world opened up to me spiritually, mentally, and emotionally. Another thing I noticed was that when I stepped into this portal, time itself seemed to come to a complete and total standstill; it became eternity. How I knew this, I do not know. It was something I simply knew without any shadow of doubt. Virtual truths began to flood my innermost being. As I stood in this light, things that I could not possibly have any way of knowing were imparted into my soul supernaturally.

As a result of this experience, I believe that my spiritual growth was accelerated beyond all natural reason. The proof of this is that the last 40 years God has allowed me to go places and do things I could never have done on my own strength or ability. This is not the first time in history something like this has transpired. Solomon is a good example. God supernaturally imparted into Solomon understanding and wisdom that he would never have attained through natural means. (We might call this a "Divine download" into Solomon.) Read the book of proverbs.

"And God gave Solomon wisdom and understanding exceeding much, and largeness of heart, even as the sand that is on the sea shore. And Solomon's wisdom excelled the wisdom of all the children of the east country, and all the wisdom of Egypt. For he was wiser than all men; than Ethan the Ezrahite, and Heman, and Chalcol, and Darda, the sons of Mahol: and his fame was in all nations round about. And he spake three thousand proverbs: and his songs were a thousand and five. And he spake of trees, from the cedar tree that is in Lebanon even unto the hyssop that springeth out of the wall: he spake also of beasts, and of fowl, and of creeping things, and of fishes. And there came of all people to hear the wisdom of Solomon, from all kings of the earth, which had heard of his wisdom" (1 Kings 4:29-34).

Brain-Quickening Experience

In about 1994 the Lord basically told me that I was a "favorite scripture" preacher, and that I really did not know his Word the way I should. I was so convicted by this confrontation from God that I made a commitment that when I got home I would begin to pour myself into the Bible like I should. I was going to spend hours in God's Word and prayer.

I informed my staff that I would begin to give myself to long hours of prayer and the Word. I began with the book of Ephesians, starting with the very first chapter. I did not want to only memorize it, but I wanted to get it into my heart. This took me close to three weeks and countless hours to memorize.

Then the next mountain I climbed was the book of Galatians. As I was memorizing scriptures and chapters of the Bible, I would get tremendous headaches. But I kept working at it because I knew that without pain, there is no gain.

When I had conquered the book of Galatians, I moved to Philippians. As I was into the second chapter of the book of Philippians, something supernatural happened took place. I had what the Bible calls an open vision. This happens when you are wide awake and everything disappears except what God is showing you. There in front of me was a large body of water. It was pure blue with not one ripple upon it, stretching as far as the natural eye could see in every direction. The room I was in was gone and there was nothing but this gigantic blue lake. As I lifted my head to look into the light blue cloudless sky, a large, crystal-clear rain drop came falling down in slow motion from the heavens. I watched in amazement as it slowly came tumbling down towards this lake. When it hit the surface of this body of water, it caused ripples to flow forth.

These ripples, as they flowed forth from the center of where the drop had hit, began to grow in size and intensity. Then all of a sudden, the vision was over. I stood there in amazement, not understanding what had just happened. I knew this experience was from God, but I did not know what its significance was.

I knew in my heart that God eventually would show me what it meant. You see, when the Lord gives me a supernatural visitation, I do not lean to the understanding of my natural mind. I just simply give it to the Lord, knowing that in His time He will show me what He meant, or what He was saying.

I picked up my Bible to get back to my memorizing scriptures. I immediately noticed that there was a change in my mental capacity. It seemed like as if my brain was absorbing the Word of God like a sponge. Within one hour I memorized a whole chapter, as if it were nothing. To my amazement, my brain had become almost photogenic. Where it took me days to memorize a chapter before, now I could memorize a chapter in an hour. I continued to memorize books of the Bible until there were ten books inside of me. This is not including thousands of other scriptures that I continued to memorize dealing with certain subjects. (I have videos on YouTube where I quote whole Epistles by memory)

Why in the world would God open up my heart and my mind the way He did to memorize the Word. The Word of God has the capacity to quicken our minds and mortal bodies. God's Word is awesome, quick and powerful. I believe that there is an activation of the things of the Spirit, when we begin to give one hundred percent into whatever it is that God has called us to do. There is a dynamic principle of laying your life down, in order to release the aroma of heaven.

I'm sorry to say, though, that I became so busy running the church, Christian school, a small bible college, radio station, TV broadcasting and construction projects, twenty-five churches in the

Philippines, not including other aspects of being a pastor, that I did not continue in memorizing the Bible.

Through the years though, I've had an insatiable hunger for the Word of God. God has allowed me to write over seven thousand sermons, 30 books, and to do many things that I never have been taught or trained to do. In the midst of all these activities I have earned a PhD in biblical theology and I received a Doctorate of Divinity. I believe it is all because of the divine supernatural visitations and quickening's of God's Holy Spirit. The reason why I believe we do not experience more of these visitations is because of a lack of spiritual hunger. If we would hunger and thirst, God would satisfy these desires.

"Blessed are they which do hunger and thirst after righteousness: for they shall be filled" (Matt 5:6).

"Delight thyself also in the LORD; and he shall give thee the desires of thine heart. Commit thy way unto the LORD; trust also in him; and he shall bring it to pass. And he shall bring forth thy righteousness as the light, and thy judgment as the noonday" (Ps. 37:4-6).

Tunnel of Light

The light in this tunnel was just as bright, but it no longer hurt my eyes. Before me laid a seemingly never- ending corridor. The walls, floor, and ceiling of this tunnel were made of tangible light. I was literally walking on or in a beam of light. The walls and floor were actually real. This long corridor of light seemed to be headed upward on a slight incline toward the heavens. The angel and I began to walk up this long corridor together with him holding my hand as if I was a little child. We seemed to walk together like this forever. It felt like a never-ending walk, yet I never got tired or weary. Actually it was an extremely pleasant walk. After what appeared to be a noticeable length of time the angelic being just disappeared. I did not know exactly when he disappeared. One minute he was at my side, and the next minute I realized he was gone. At the same time I did not feel disappointed, or upset that he was gone. I just knew in my heart that this was the will of God. Not knowing what else to do, I kept on walking.

Now even though the angel was no longer with me, I did not feel all alone for I could sense that God was right there at my side, maybe not in the physical form but by His spiritual overwhelming presence. Something else strange was happening. Even though I was walking at a normal pace, it seemed like I was moving extremely fast. It was like I was on a high-speed escalator. It makes me laugh now, but I think I was going at the speed of light. At the same time both my mind and heart were experiencing an overwhelming peace and joy. There were no fears, cares, sin, or sorrow, just total harmony and serenity of spirit, soul, mind, and body. All of my past was gone as if it never existed. All of the struggles and wrestling, fears and anxieties, were gone. It was absolute heavenly bliss. I cannot describe how incredible I felt. In all of my imaginations I never thought someone could feel as good as I was feeling. In hell there is nothing but pain and suffering. But in heaven there is nothing but pleasure and awesome peace.

CHAPTER FOUR
Garden of Eden

The next thing I knew; I was out of this tunnel of light, and I found myself standing on a tall hill covered with emerald green grass. I had entered into a place so beautiful and incredible that it temporarily took my breath away. There, stretched out before me as far as my eyes could see, was a majestic and indescribable world. Right below me was the most perfect valley you could ever imagine. What I was looking upon is beyond the comprehension of human description or understanding. There were snow-capped mountains just off to the left of me in the far distance, rolling hills to the right, and the valley that was below me was amazingly picturesque. In this valley was a beautiful river. In the distance straight ahead of me there was an incredible forest filled with trees greater than the redwoods in California.

"But as it is written, Eye hath not seen, nor ear heard, neither have entered into the heart of man, the things which God hath prepared for them that love him. But God hath revealed them unto us by his Spirit: for the Spirit searcheth all things, yea, the deep things of God"(1 Cor. 2:9-10).

Everywhere I looked there was an abundance of life! There were plants, animals, and insects. God is the Creator and Author of all life. Just by what He has created, you can tell He loves creativity and He loves life! In the first two chapters of Genesis we get a glimpse of God's perfect will. I almost laugh every time somebody questions whether or not there could be life on other planets. If the Lord should tarry and we would have an opportunity to thoroughly examine the heavenly bodies, we will discover life even on asteroids. Granted it may be microscopic, but it would still be life. I could even believe that there is life living in the vacuum of space itself.

"And God saw everything that he had made, and, behold, it was very good. And the evening and the morning were the sixth day" (Gen. 1:31).

The grass upon the hill and much of the valley was a deep emerald green. It was the perfect length, not too short and not too high. Across the valley I could see wheat fields blowing in the wind. Upon the hillsides and plains were beautiful flowers growing in perfect uniformity, as if a gardener with the most exquisite taste had planted each and every one of them exactly what they needed to be. There were amazing, beautiful bushes and hedges as well as plants of every description, size, and shape. Even though through the years I have loved and enjoyed nature, I have never been one to really memorize the names and types of trees, flowers, and plants. The mass majority of the things I saw I could not give you names for, but they were everywhere in abundance.

As I said, in the distance I could see that there was a large forest of trees that were gigantic in proportion. These were redwoods, but they were taller and wider than the redwood forests in Oregon or California, reaching towards the heavens above them. I have lived in California and Oregon, and there is no denying the beauty of the redwood forests located there. And yet there is absolutely no comparison between these redwood trees and the ones that are there.

All the plants, animals, and everything I beheld were absolutely perfect in their beauty and completeness. The greatest artist that has ever lived could never imagine what I was now seeing and experiencing.

As I gazed across the landscape, I saw animals large and small, too numerous to count. There were deer, rabbits, and lions eating grass. A small family of bears was splashing in the river, which seemed almost transparent. This river flowed down from a snow-white mountain range unlike any on earth. It was almost like a zoo, but with none of the cages and fences to keep you separated from the animals. It may sound like it was crowded with the description I am sharing with you, but this was not the case. All of the animal and plant life was scattered across the horizon in such an amazing and splendid picturesque way. The river that tumbled its way down the mountainside created waterfalls here and there, until it found its way down to the valley seeking the lowest place of gravity. As the water fell from the side of this mountain, it created a half a dozen or so multicolored rainbows that stood out as if they were three-dimensional.

I have no words to describe the beauty of which I was seeing. I stood frozen in place, overcome with what lay in front of me. I was in a garden that must have been very similar to the Garden of Eden in the book of Genesis. Of course it has not been inhabited by the human race since they were expelled from it. Two cherubim were assigned to stand before its gates. They were to bar the entrance of man from coming back into the garden, in order to prevent him from eating of the tree of life.

"Therefore the LORD God sent him forth from the garden of Eden, to till the ground from whence he was taken. So he drove out the man; and he placed at the east of the garden of Eden Cherubims, and a flaming sword which turned every way, to keep the way of the tree of life" (Gen. 3:23-24).

Once we leave Earth as God's people, not only is the Garden of Eden opened to us again but also the tree of life. During my experience I did not see another human being in this place or even any signs that there were people living there. Yet I was not lonely in any aspect of the word. The very air was permeated with such an overwhelming reality of God. The Holy Spirit had to be enabling me to continue to stand upon my feet, otherwise I surely would have fallen on my face because of the awesomeness of God's presence.

"Then I arose, and went forth into the plain: and, behold, the glory of the LORD stood there, as the glory which I saw by the river of Chebar: and I fell on my face" (Ezek. 3:23).

"And when I saw him, I fell at his feet as dead. And he laid his right hand upon me, saying unto me, Fear not; I am the first and the last" (Rev. 1:17).

Animal Kingdom

Botanists are scientists who study plants. Zoologists are those who study animals. Naturalists study animals, plants, humans, and nature. Herpetologists study reptiles and amphibians.

Ichthyologists study fish. And Entomologists study insects and spiders.

The reason I bring up the names of these specialists is because if they would have been there with me, they would've had the time of their lives. They would have seen all the wonders of Earth's absolute perfection.

Biologists today generally classify all living things into five kingdoms. Two of these are the familiar plant and animal kingdoms. The other three are comprised mainly of very small organisms, like bacteria, larger single- celled creatures, and fungi. The animal kingdom has by far the most species, well over a million. There are over four hundred thousand known plant species, most of which are flowering plants with seeds, such as trees, grasses, and the like. The latter comprise more than a quarter of a million different species. The other three kingdoms contain at least a few hundred thousand different life forms.

The animal kingdom is divided into about thirty phyla. The nine largest phyla contain the majority of species. Indeed, one phyla, the arthropods, which includes insects and spiders, constitutes about 75 percent of all known animal species. More than nine hundred thousand arthropods have been described, and according to some estimates there may be more than five million more.

The number of known species for all animals other than arthropods is about 250,000. The largest group (formally "class") within the phyla of arthropods and the most diverse class in all kingdoms, is insects. Over 750,000 have been described. Some suppose that there are perhaps as many as three million different species of insects in the world.

The most diverse family of insect is beetles, with over 375,000 types identified. Other large families of insects include butterflies and moths (more than one hundred thousand species), bees and wasps (more than twenty thousand species), and ants (about ten thousand species). With over thirty thousand known species, spiders, which are not insects, constitute one of the large families of other kinds of arthropods. Only two other phyla within the animal kingdom, the roundworms and the mollusks, are known to contain more than one hundred thousand species. All other phyla generally have far less.

The dominant phyla on the planet, the vertebrates, consists of less than fifty thousand known species. The number of fish species is estimated to be more than twenty thousand, bird species number approximately 8,700, reptiles about 6,000, mammals about 4,500, and amphibians about 2,500. Within mammals, the rodents are the most varied order, with thirty-four families and more than 1,700 species. 20

I am sharing this scientific information with you to help expand your horizon that you might better understand who God really is. God is so creative and so full of life that there is no end to His creative ability. These are all natural things that we can discover with the human eye. What myriad of angels, angelic beings, and spiritual beings exist that we cannot see or perceive? Millions? Billions? Trillions? Who can say? From my study of the Scriptures I have discovered at least ten different types of angels. This is by no means meant to be in any way, form, or fashion a complete list.

1.Cherubim: Genesis 3:24; Ezekiel 1:5-28; 28:12, 13, 17; 8:1-4; 10:1-22

2.Seraphim: Isaiah 6:1-7

3.Archangels: Colossians 1:15-18; 1 Thessalonians 4:16; Jude 9

4.Common angels: Matthew 1:20-29; 2:13-19; 28:2- 5; Acts 5:19; 8:26; 10:3; 12:7

5.Guardian angels: Psalm 91:12

6.Ministering angels: 1 Kings 19:5-7

7.Avenging angels: Genesis 19:1-29

8.Death angels: Exodus 12:23; Revelation 6:8

9.Living creatures: Revelation 4:6-5:14; 6:1-8; 7:11; 14:3, 9-11; 15:7; 19:4

10.Messengers: similar to the one that came to me!

Many people have questions about animals. What happens to animals when they die? Do animals have souls? Almost every question I believe that we have pertaining to life is found within the Scriptures. All we need is to rightly divide the Word of truth by the Holy Spirit. First we understand the animals came from the earth.

"And God said, Let the earth bring forth the living creature after his kind, cattle, and creeping thing, and beast of the earth after his kind: and it was so. And God made the beast of the earth after his kind, and cattle after their kind, and everything that creepeth upon the earth after his kind: and God saw that it was good" (Gen. 1:24-25).

The following Scripture would imply that the spirit (the soul) of an animal returns to the earth from whence it came:

"Who knoweth the spirit of man that goeth upward, and the spirit of the beast that goeth downward to the earth?" (Eccles. 3:21).

All animals belong to God and are made for His pleasure.

"For every beast of the forest is mine, and the cattle upon a thousand hills. I know all the fowls of the mountains: and the wild beasts of the field are mine" (Ps. 50:10-11).

Divine Orchestra

In this place called heaven, my hearing had become extremely sensitive. I had been so overwhelmed by what I was seeing, it had escaped my attention what I was also hearing. My ears seemed to be able to pick up sounds that were miles away. Not only could I hear everything, but also I could distinguish every sound. I literally could hear the bees going from one flower to another collecting pollen. I heard a slight breeze blowing through the grass on the plains and a cow and its calf chewing their cud. A lion in the distance roared, not with the ferociousness of a vicious meat eater but of a lion that was relishing its existence in harmony with its other fellow creatures. I could even hear rabbits skipping across the grass. I heard all of these distinct individual sounds, yet it was not annoying or confusing like the mad rushing about that goes on in the cities of men. It sounded more like a beautiful orchestra being conducted by a divinely gifted maestro. Such a symphony has never been heard upon Earth since the fall of man.

Supernatural Eyesight

At almost the same time, I noticed the vibrant and vivid colors. They were of such deepness, clarity, and brilliance. Everything was astonishingly three- dimensional. All of the artistic geniuses of this day and age could never even create on paper anything as near to perfection as this was. After this supernatural experience, everything in this world seems to be dim and surreal to me. We may not be able to realize the fullest capacity at this moment, but the spiritual world is more real than the physical world that we live in.

Not only was there incredible supernatural clarity to my sight and hearing but also to my sense of smell, taste, and touch. It all seemed to be magnified a thousand fold. If you could compare these two worlds side-by-side, it would reveal the blandness, the ugliness of the natural world we live in. It is all because of the corruption of sin. The satanic seed that says "my will be done."

But this place of glorious beauty simply revealed the exquisiteness of all that God had created. The aromas that floated in the atmosphere filled my nostrils. The smells were very strong but not at all nauseating; it was quite the opposite. I could even taste to some degree through the sense of my smell. It was one of many delightful experiences that I was encountering in this heavenly place. All of these things registered in my mind, and I knew that I was in heaven. In all of my imaginations of what heaven would be like, never once did it occur to me that it would be like this. Revelation knowledge flowed through my soul as I came to realize God's original plan for man. The earth was to be a miniature version of God's divine habitation. But man's rebellion, his disobedience in yielding his soul to Satan, opened the door to disaster, pestilence, disease, perversion, and corruption. Which turned the earth into a tragic mockery of God's original plan. What was meant to be heaven on earth had become a hellish nightmare.

Dr Michael H Yeager

CHAPTER FIVE

Upon a New Road

While pondering these thoughts, I noticed that there was a road that wound its way down through the valley. It was headed in the direction of the gigantic redwood forest. Instinctively my feet began to move me down the hill toward this road. When I finally arrived at it, I looked back from where I came from and realized that I had walked miles and miles. Amazingly, I felt just as relaxed as when I first began, if not even more so. When I reached this road, I discovered that it was built with beautiful multi-colored flat stones, intricately laid together side by side. These stones look like highly polished marble filled with many gold speckles. The road glistened and simmered as if it was wet and slippery. Yet when I stepped upon it I discovered that it was not slippery or wet at all. There were quite a number of different types of animals alongside as well as on the road. None of them fled from me as I walked past them. It was as if all creation was in complete harmony, and I was not a stranger. Rather, I was an intricate an intimate part of this heavenly place. There was absolutely no fear toward me in these animals that I walked past. Neither was there any fear whatsoever in my heart toward them.

It would've been so wonderful to stop and spend some time petting and playing with these animals. It also would have been nice to walk down through the meadows, to sit by the bank of the beautiful river that was flowing not too far from the road just to let my feet soak in the crystal clear waters. It would have been wonderful to sit down and watch all of the different types of fish that were probably swimming in this crystal-clear river. If only I could just stay right there forever.

Yet there was a deep urgency in my heart. There was something that must transpire while I was there. I knew I was not there just for a foretaste of the future. That God had brought me to this place to show me something pertaining to my purpose in life and humanity was certain. I knew instinctively that what God wanted to show me was somewhere along this road that I was walking upon. I finally reached this majestic forest of redwood trees. The tops of these trees must have been reaching anywhere from two hundred to three hundred feet in the air. There were also smaller trees scattered throughout these giants of the forest. Their circumferences were anywhere from three feet to forty feet in dimension. It was simply mind-boggling.

I stepped into this forest walking upon the multi- colored road. As I came under the towering canopy of these trees, I felt myself being enfolded and wrapped up with comfort and security. How can I describe what I was experiencing at that moment? Without being misunderstood I would like to say that it was magical and mystical. Walt Disney himself would be blown away. None of his children's movies ever came close to what I was experiencing now. Light filtered down through the branches here and there causing shimmering reflections of light to shine off of the leaves of other trees that were growing under the huge canopy. The ground, tree trunks, and large rocks and boulders were covered with many colors of moss. The moss was exquisitely placed as if by professional design. Ferns, some large and many small, stretched through the forest in perfect arrangement. I did not see any thistles or thorns. This place had never experienced the curse of sin.

The path led straight into the heart of the forest. There were no bends or turns as far as my eyes could see. It was as straight as an arrow flies. I walked down this path at an easy rate taking in as much as I could. It was as if I was walking on a cloud. It seemed to be dreamlike and yet it was tangible and touchable. Once in a while, there would be a stone bridge on the path. The stone bridges were made of the same stones as the road itself. The bridges took me over bubbling, sparkling, and transparent water. At one of these streams I stopped for a moment and looked over the bridge into the water. As I looked into the water I could see schools of fish swimming by. They were bright and beautiful like coral reef fish back on Earth, but they were much more exquisite and stunning. The water was so clear that it looked like the fish were swimming in the air. As I continued to walk, my heart overflowed with love for the One who created all of this. As I recall this account, I still get spiritual chills flowing through me.

How far and how long I walked I could not guess. I do know that it was long enough to expect that the sun would be going down. However, there was no change in the light. It was just as bright as when I had first arrived. As I reflected upon this wonder, it dawned upon me that I had not seen the sun in the sky. That the light seemed to be coming from nowhere and yet everywhere! This light did not hurt my eyes. Actually, it was as if my eyes were drinking deep of the light. It was extremely strange and delightful. My eyes were absorbing and pulling in this wonderful light.

The Birds of Heaven

As I continued to walk, everything was so amazingly peaceful and tranquil. Majestic trees stood to the left and right of the approximately twenty-foot wide path. I found myself praising and worshiping God. I discovered that God also had transformed my voice. I could hardly believe how good I could sing. And with this new voice I began to sing with all of my heart my love for the One who meant everything. I was so at home, at peace, and in harmony with this place that I never wanted to leave. I belonged here. I knew I was made to live here forever, that this was my natural environment. As I continued to walk, sing, and worship, the trees began to be filled with birds, thousands upon thousands of birds. The light filtering in between the trees glistened on these birds which were of such magnificent beauty and variety.

There were large and small birds of colors and species beyond count. Cockatoos, canaries, doves, parakeets, and finches came just to name a few. Their voices echoed throughout the forest. I knew in my heart that they were singing praises to God. It made you want to be able to join in with them. As I kept on walking, I was completely and totally surrounded by them. It was so overwhelming that I could not walk any further. I just stood there caught up in the majesty and the beauty of it all. They were all lifting their voices in praise, worship, adoration, and love for the Author of life.

Divine Commission

I was so caught up in the wonder and beauty of it all that I did not even notice the angel who had been with me at the start of this journey had returned. He was standing alongside me, gazing at the birds in the trees. The angel asked, **"Do you see all of these**

splendid and beautiful birds?" Surprisingly, I was not at all startled or surprised by the return of this angel. In heaven there is no fear, sickness, or sin. There is nothing but joy, peace, and tranquility beyond description. I turned and spoke to the angel not as a superior but as a fellow companion in the plan and purposes of God. "Sir," I said, "Do you not think that these birds are the most beautiful and amazing creatures you have ever heard or seen?" The angel asked, **"Do you understand what it is the Lord God is revealing to you?"** When the angel said this to me, I turned once again and looked up directly into his face. I said to him, "What do you mean?" And then this angel said something to me that still overwhelms me to this day. As I share this part of my experience with you, I am almost to the point of weeping. Deep, deep feelings are stirring and moving in my heart. For God was about to reveal His divine commission for my life, the purpose for which Jesus rescued me.

"These birds you are looking upon and listening to are a type, and a shadow of those things which will come to be in and through your life. Even as these birds are of so many different species and colors, so in your future will you have an impact upon many cultures and tongues and nations."

At this statement my mind seemed to go numb for a moment. It just did not seem to make sense. I remember saying, "I don't understand what you mean." He replied, "Servant of the Most High, be it known to you that what you see is a shadow of the souls of men and women who will be brought into the kingdom because of your obedience and hunger for the Lord. Many will be set free from the bondage of sin. Multitudes of many nations, tongues, and tribes will hear the glorious truth, and this truth will set them free. They in turn will go forth in the power and presence of the Holy Spirit and will take the name of Jesus, even as you have done and will do. They will drive back the forces of the adversary. For the day of the Lord is at hand, and a new day is about to dawn. Strengthen your heart. Be strong in the Lord and the power of His might. Hold up the arms of your brethren; wash their feet. Humble yourself. Be a servant, and the Lord will use you. Help those who are called and chosen but have none to assist them. Undergird and encourage them to fulfill the call of God upon their lives."

The words of this messenger of God penetrated my heart to its deepest core. I fell to my knees, then to my face, crying and weeping uncontrollably. **God had spoken to me**. I would never be the same again! The Lord did have a divine purpose for my life. I was called of God and sent forth by the Almighty to set others free. Instantly, in my heart I knew that it was not about me. I knew that I was only one small gear in the majestic machinery of God's divine plan. My heart was filled with joy unspeakable and full of glory. How long I lay there on that road and cried and wept, I do not know. The next thing I realized was that the angel was gone, and I was no longer in the woods.

CHAPTER SIX
Before the Throne

Next I found myself in an immense never-ending realm. So large was this place that I could not see an ending. Above me, behind me, to the left and the right just seemed to be a never-ending horizon. The floor under my feet was like a sea of crystal glass radiating and pulsating with ever-changing colors that flowed through it like an incoming wave of the ocean. In the distance, I saw lightning and extremely bright flashes of light proceeding from one point. Not knowing what else to do, I began to move toward this phenomenon. As I drew closer, I heard thunder echoing off in the distance which sounded like mighty trumpets. The sea of glass under my feet shook with every peel of lightning. And with every step I took toward this phenomenon, my heart beat faster. It was as if the hair on the back of my neck and up my arms and head were standing straight up.

In the far distance I could see that I was approaching what looked like a huge throne. In front of the throne and around it, there seemed to be some type of activity that was transpiring. As I got closer I began to discern the most awesome creatures I could have ever imagine. Yet my attention was not on them. The Scriptures declare that there are four of them altogether, full of eyes before and behind. The first is like a lion, the second like a calf, the third has the face of a man, and the fourth beast is like a flying eagle. They each have six wings and on the inside of the wings they are full of eyes. When I was still a great way off, even before I saw them, I heard these beasts declaring with a loud voice, "Holy, holy, holy, Lord God Almighty, Who was and Who is and Who is to come." (Up to this point many of these things I am relating to you seemed to have vanished from my mind)

I only had eyes for the One on the throne. I could tell that the throne was amazing, but even more majestic and splendid than the throne was the One who sat upon it. He appeared like the brightness of translucent diamonds. A light shined out of the One on the throne that was of such an intensity and holiness. Had I not been in the spirit, it would have killed me, consumed me, burned me up, and evaporated me into nothingness. At the right side sat Jesus, clothed with a robe down to His feet, and about His chest He had a breastplate of glistening gold like that of a Roman general. His hair radiated like glistening white wool, more pure than the whitest snow. His eyes burned with divine love as if flames of fire. Streaks of lightning were flashing all around the throne. The roar of thunder continued.

"And in the midst of the seven candlesticks one like unto the Son of man, clothed with a garment down to the foot, and girt about the paps with a golden girdle. His head and his hairs were white like wool, as white as snow; and his eyes were as a flame of fire;

And his feet like unto fine brass, as if they burned in a furnace; and his voice as the sound of many waters. And he had in his right hand seven stars: and out of his mouth went a sharp two edged sword: and his countenance was as the sun shineth in his strength" (Rev. 1:13-16).

Before the Throne

I knew without a shadow of doubt that I stood before God the Father and His Son, Jesus Christ. Around about them and stretching over the top of them shone numerous emerald rainbows much clearer and colorful than the natural mind could conceive.

"After this I looked, and, behold, a door was opened in heaven: and the first voice which I heard was as it were of a trumpet talking with me; which said, Come up hither, and I will shew thee things which must be hereafter. And immediately I was in the spirit: and, behold, a throne was set in heaven, and one sat on the throne. And he that sat was to look upon like a jasper and a sardine stone: and there was a rainbow round about the throne, in sight like unto an emerald. And round about the throne were four and twenty seats: and upon the seats I saw four and twenty elders sitting, clothed in white raiment; and they had on their heads crowns of gold. And out of the throne proceeded lightnings and thunderings and voices: and there were seven lamps of fire burning before the throne, which are the seven Spirits of God. And before the throne there was a sea of glass like unto crystal: and in the midst of the throne, and round about the throne, were four beasts full of eyes before and behind. And the first beast was like a lion, and the second beast like a calf, and the third beast had a face as a man, and the fourth beast was like a flying eagle. And the four beasts had each of them six wings

about him; and they were full of eyes within: and they rest not day and night, saying, Holy, holy, holy, Lord God Almighty, which was, and is, and is to come. And when those beasts give glory and honour and thanks to him that sat on the throne, who liveth for ever and ever, The four and twenty elders fall down before him that sat on the throne, and worship him that liveth for ever and ever, and cast their crowns before the throne, saying, Thou art worthy, O Lord, to receive glory and honour and power: for thou hast created all things, and for thy pleasure they are and were created" (Rev. 4:1-11).

I fell as one dead before the throne, quivering and shaking before the presence of my Lord. Then a voice spoke forth as if coming from everywhere. It filled my mind and heart with shaking and trembling. This voice was filled with absolute complete and total authority and holiness. I knew it was the **Father's voice** that was speaking to me. As I lay on my face before the throne of God, I heard unspeakable words that could not be uttered with human vocabulary. It was literally as if streaks of lightning were hitting my body with every word that He spoke. As His words hit my body they would explode in me like the soundings of thunder. My whole body literally shook and vibrated uncontrollably at these thundering's. These thundering's flooded my body and took a hold of me. It had to be God supernaturally strengthening me in order to keep me alive through this experience.

I am convinced that if you had been standing at a distance you would have seen streaks of divine lightning and fire striking my body. This divine lightning and fire was not meant to destroy me but to some extent was meant to impregnate me with God's divine purposes and abilities.

I knew that my inner man was drinking deep of the mysteries and divine plans of God. I remember the tears flowing from my eyes, down my face as I listened to the Word of the Lord. The glory of God was all around, upon, and in me. My body was enveloped in a glistening cloud of energy. Through this whole experience I laid there weeping and whispering "Thank you, Jesus," over and over. I did not truly understand with my mind what was transpiring, but I knew in my heart that God was speaking to me divine truths and mysteries, that which was to be accomplished and would shortly come to pass. I knew that He was supernaturally imparting into me the grace that was necessary to accomplish His purposes for my life. This seemed to go on forever. Then as quickly as it had started it was over. The Spirit of the Lord whisked me instantly away from the throne room of God.

Preaching the Gospel

The next place I found myself was on a sidewalk in what looked to be an alleyway of a low-income area of a large city. Coming down the street toward me were two large, rough-looking men. As they caught up to me, I found myself sharing the love and the Good News of Jesus Christ. I also shared the reality of divine judgment if they rejected the sacrificial work of Jesus. As I continued to speak about the reality of Christ and that there is no other way to the Father but through Jesus, I noticed their faces begin to distort until they were filled with absolute, utter hate. Their eyes glistened with a hideous satanic appearance as if they were turning into demons right before my eyes. Before I could even raise my hands in self-defense, they began to hit me in the face and the chest with their fists. After numerous blows, I finally fell to my knees. As I did, they kicked and stomped down on me. In the midst of this persecution, no hatred or malice emanated from my heart for these men that were trying to kill me. My heart and my mind seemed to be completely floating in a sea of love and peace. I found myself crying out loud for them. "Father, please forgive them, for they do not know what they are doing." And then everything went completely black.

When I came to, I found myself lying on the floor of my barracks. I looked around the room expecting to see the angel, but there was no one there but me. It was late in the afternoon. I think approximately at least five hours had come and gone since the angel had first appeared. My experience was not a dream. The reality of everything that had transpired is still eternally embodied in my mind and my heart. I can see it all as clearly as if it had just happened. Whether or not I was in my body or out of it, I cannot tell. I can say this though: without a shadow of a doubt, God has placed a divine mission in my life to complete, a job to do, a purpose to fulfill. By God's grace, nothing will rob me of the reality of it. With all my might, I am determined to fulfill God's will for my life. By God's grace I am not going to disappoint the One who has chosen me to be a soldier in His last day army. I hope you understand that you also have a divine mission and purpose in this life. I pray to God that you will be faithful to that divine call.

"And from the days of John the Baptist until now the kingdom of heaven suffereth violence, and the violent take it by force" (Matt. 11:12).

CHAPTER SEVEN
THE DREAM

This is the third visitation I would like to share with you. I had an amazing dream recently. It's very hard to describe in human vernacular. I was sleeping peacefully when, at about three o'clock in the morning, I was suddenly smack dab in the middle of heaven, close to the throne of God. It was so real and tangible; it literally felt as if I was in heaven physically. God gave me eyes to see all of existence. It was as if I was omnipresent. All of creation lay before me. My mind and emotions, and all five of my senses perceived all things. I embraced everything at one time.

It was the most amazing experience you could imagine. It was so beautiful and magnificent that it is beyond precise description. It could be likened to being in the eye of a storm with everything spinning around you. With this supernatural, imparted ability I could perceive the spiritual and angelic. I saw angels of all types and ranks. I saw and felt the nature and the physical realms. I saw the planets, moons, stars, solar systems, and the whole universe. I saw animal life, plant life, oceans, seas, lakes, and rivers. I even saw the microscopic molecular realm. God supernaturally expanded my capacity mentally and emotionally to perceive all things. If it had not happened to me personally, I would be skeptical myself of someone saying these things.

In the midst of this experience I began to be overtaken by an absolute sense of incredible harmony. It was a unity and oneness of a mind-boggling proportion. It resonated through my whole being. I could feel it in my bones, flesh, emotions, and mind. My heart resonated with His harmony. My whole being was engulfed in this unbelievable symphony. All creation, the universe, and spiritual realm was in complete and total harmony and unity. Instantly I perceived everything was at one with God. Not one molecule, not one atom or proton was out of sync with God. As I was looking at creation, suddenly I perceived an invisible force permeating and saturating all of it. God literally gave me eyes to see this invisible force. I could see it moving, flowing, and penetrating everything. With this ability to see, He also gave me spiritual understanding. I realized at that moment that it was this incredible invisible force which was causing all things to exist and flow and move as one living, breathing creation.

What I am sharing with you was a progressive revelation unfolding before me like a flower blossoming. In the midst of this experience my ears opened, and I heard the most incredible music, a breathtaking song. This invisible force was literally a song that was being sung. Instantly I perceived that it was this music, this song, which was holding all of creation together. This song was permeating every animate and inanimate thing together. Not only was it holding everything together but also everything was singing along with it. It was the most incredible music and song you could ever imagine. Actually it is beyond comprehension or human ability to describe this song and what it was doing. All of creation was being upheld and kept together by this song. I could see it and feel it. It was inside of me. I was a part of it. No maestro, psalmist, no Beethoven or Mozart could ever produce such a majestic masterpiece.

As I watched and listened, I was overwhelmed with the reality that it was this song that was causing everything to be in harmony and unity. It was this song causing everything to live, move, exist, and have being. During this experience a curiosity took a hold of me. I began to wonder, where is this music, this song, coming from? I began to look high and low, trying to discover where this song had originated. I finally looked behind me, and on a higher elevation I saw God sitting upon His throne. I did not see the clarity of God's form or face. He was covered in a glistening mist, somewhat like fog. But as I looked upon His form, it was as if my eyes zoomed in on His mouth. I was looking intently at the mouth of God. Out of His mouth was coming this amazing, beautiful, awesome song.

This song that God was singing was holding everything together and in perfect harmony. God the Father was making everything one with Himself through this song, this music coming out of His mouth. I literally could see, feel, and experience the song coming out of God's mouth. In my heart I said to the Father, "Father, how long will You sing this song?" And He spoke to me in my heart, "Throughout eternity, My voice will never cease to sing. My voice will never cease to be heard." I could see letters streaming from God's mouth. Words were coming forth from His mouth. They were swimming in a river of transparent life, like fish swimming in a river. These words seemed to be alive. They were spreading throughout the entire universe, causing everything to exist and to be in harmony. They were permeating all of creation, visible and invisible, spiritual and natural.

I knew in my heart that this was the Word of God, the divinely inspired Scriptures. The Word was swimming as if in an invisible transparent river. I knew that this river was a living, quickening force. I knew that it was this river which was causing the Word of God to be alive. The Word of God was being carried forth by this river. I said to the Father, "Father, what is this river that the Word is flowing, swimming, and living in?" And He said to my heart, "It is the Holy Ghost!"

I was stunned into silence. After a while I repeated my question. Once again He said to me, "It is the Holy Ghost. It is the breath of My mouth coming from the voice of My lips. And this voice is My Son, Jesus Christ. My voice is My Son, Jesus Christ. And out of His voice comes the Holy Ghost and My Word." Further He said to me, "My Word would not sustain, heal, deliver, or bring life unless it is quickened and made alive by My Spirit." Then the Father confirmed this to me by quoting the Scripture where Jesus said, *"My Words are Spirit, and they are life." (See John 6:63.)* The Father spoke to me again and said, "You can quote, memorize, and declare the whole Bible, but it will be dead and lifeless until you yield, surrender, move, flow, and come into complete harmony with the Word of God and the Holy Ghost."

This I believe, to some extent, reveals God's eternal purpose for you and I: to be in complete oneness and harmony with God, the Father, the Son, and the Holy Ghost!

CHAPTER EIGHT
A SIGNIFICANT VISITATION

(From my book: **The Coming Great Awakening**)

I would like to share with you the fourth amazing visitation that I had on February the 20, 2012. On the 18 of February, I celebrated my 56th birthday. The 37th year of being born again and having been a pastor since 1977. I set my heart to seek God, trusting to totally separate my mind and my heart free from all useless knowledge. Giving myself over to nothing but God's Word, and only the information which I needed in order to fulfill the will of God for my life. From the minute I set my mind and heart to be completely given over to the Lord, great anticipation and expectation began to rise in me. On the third day I went to bed meditating upon God's WORD. The dream I am about to share with you was more than a dream. All of my five senses and physical being experienced that which I am about to share.

In this Dream I found myself standing outside of a small town on top of a grass covered hill. Other saints (some that I am familiar with) were gathered together there with me. (There were seven to a dozen of us). The stars were shining brightly from above. There was no moon this particular night. It was a beautiful warm summer evening. You could hear the night life all around us. The crickets and frogs were joined together in their song. As I was standing there with the gathering of these saints, I sensed in my heart that something astounding was about to happen in the heavens above us.

I perceived that the heavens were about to be shaken. I perceived in my heart that it was necessary for all of us to immediately get on our backs, and look into the heavens. When I shared this with those who were gathered together with me on the Hill, they all agreed and we immediately laid down on our backs. Within just a matter of minutes the heavens above us exploded into activity. It was as if a great battle was unfolding in the heavens. There was destruction happening throughout the sky as if it was in great travail and pain, as if it was in a process of giving birth. A coming forth of a new life and a new heaven.

What we watched unfold above us was mind boggling and dumbfounding, frightening and yet exhilarating. It seemed to go on for hours, and just as fast as it had begun, it was suddenly over. All of us present slowly arose to our feet. We were so overwhelmed and dumbfounded by what we had just experienced that none of us could talk. **We were totally and utterly speechless**. Our hearts were filled with wonder and amazement. I perceived that all who were present knew that God was revealing himself to the human race in a way He had not previously demonstrated. God was doing something in the heavens and in the earth that humanity had not yet seen or heard of, or experienced.

We all dispersed from the hilltop slowly going our own separate ways. I found myself on a sidewalk beginning to enter into a small community. The streets were filled with people looking into the heavens. I could see great fear filling the faces on those who were speaking to one another in whispers about what all of this could mean? I continued to walk down the sidewalk not speaking to anyone. The atmosphere was filled with a sense of great fear and anticipation.

As I entered deeper into this town, once again I sense that something was about to happen. (Now this is where it really begins to get interesting.)The minute I perceived something dramatic was about to happen I stopped. There were tall buildings off to my right and left hand, which you would typically find in a small town.

I looked up into the heavens, and it seemed as if to me the heavens were made from a parchment. I watched in amazement as if an invisible hand was rolling up the heavens like they were a newspaper, or a parchment. And then as if the heavens were insignificant, it was set aside as if it were nothing.

The minute this took place behind where the heavens had been there was now an innumerable multitude of the heavenly host. The Saints of all ages dressed in glistening white, were gathered with the angelic armies behind them. In the midst was the Heavenly Father sitting upon a great white throne. God the Father was so huge in size that all else looked small in comparison. All of those who were present including the Father seemed to be looking off to my right.

As I looked in the direction in which they were gazing to my amazement there was the Lamb of God. His wool was glistening white as snow. He was lying upon His side as if He had been slain. His backside was away

from me, His underside toward me. And out from His rib, it seemed to be His third rib, from his side flowed a stream of bright shimmering living, quickening blood. Directly in front of His body there had formed a pool of this living blood. I knew there was no bottom to this pool of blood. It is hard to explain what I sensed in my heart as I looked upon Him, the Lamb of God, and His precious living blood.

As I was looking upon this pool of precious blood, I felt something manifest itself in my right hand. I looked down, and there in my right hand was a branch, a ROD. (This was the specific word that came to my mind)This was not just any ordinary Rod. It was absolutely straight, and it was made of Olive Wood, seemingly seven feet tall. (These are things I just knew to be true)

Immediately I knew what I was to do with this Rod in my right hand. I lifted this Rod towards the pool of blood in the heavens. To my amazement it seemed to be just the right length to reach into the blood. This blood was in the heavens, and yet this seven foot Rod was able to reach the precious blood of Jesus.

I put the end of the Rod right into this pool of living blood. The blood immediately flowed to the end of the Rod. This living blood wrapped itself around the end of the Rod as if it was in absolute oneness with the Rod. Then with my right hand I pulled the Rod back towards me. Once the Rod was back into my Realm (I do not know how else to explain it). I directed the end of the Rod towards my mouth. It looked as if the blood was

going to fall off from the end of the Rod. But not a drop fell to the ground.

I opened my mouth wide, and stuck the end of the Rod with the Living Blood into my mouth. I drank all of the blood which had been on the Rod. The very moment that I drank the blood, it was as if Power exploded inside of me, knocking me flat on my back like a dead man. It slammed me violently to the ground. I cannot properly express how drastic and violent the power of God hit me.

As I lay on the ground, my sight had become slightly dim. I saw a figure of a man walking towards me from the left. He seemed to be wearing the brown robes of a Prophet. I knew in my heart he was a Prophet. I could not see his face because there was a foggy glow that was emanating from his face. A bright light was shining from behind him. He stopped in front of me. And he said to me, **Stand upon Thy Feet O Son of Man**. The minute these words left his mouth it was like as if someone grabbed me violently by my shirt collar, and jerked me to my feet. My whole body was trembling and weak.

After I was on my feet, this Prophet held out a small wooden bowl made of acacia wood. (This word came to me in my mind) I can still see the bold white and brown grains swirling around that bowl inside and out.

The Prophet commanded me to eat of its contents. I looked into the bowl, and there in the bottom were approximately a dozen almonds. They were sliced long ways in very thin strips. They were moist and slightly green. I reached forth my right hand, because the Rod was now in my left hand. I scraped up about half of these almonds strips and stuck them into my mouth. As I completed this task the unknown Prophet turned his back on me, and walked away.

As I chewed these almonds strips they released a very bitter taste in my mouth. And as I chewed these almonds and swallowed, all that was around me suddenly disappeared. I found myself looking into the heavens again. But now there was nothing but darkness above me. The heavens were totally empty of all-stars and lights. Nothing but empty blackness as far as my eyes could see.

I noticed a motion off to my right. I saw like a small seed of light beginning to be formed. As it began to grow, I saw that it was a letter. The Letter was an **H**. as the letter **H**. continued to grow, blood was covering it, flowing into it, out of it, and through it. It was filled with the brilliant shimmering living, quickening blood of Jesus Christ. I knew that it was the blood which I had drank. This **H**. was living, active and growing.

I also noticed a motion off to my left. There in the darkness was another H. forming and growing. But this letter **H**. had a sense of evil and darkness about it. It was covered and dripping in a putrid, dead and stinking blood. As each one of these letters continued to grow, there was a separation taking place. They were growing farther and farther apart from one another. The letter **H**. to my right was filling the heavens with light, love and life. But the **H**. to my left was filled with deception, death and misery.

As I continued to watch this unfold before my eyes, suddenly the voice of God came thundering from the heavens. This is what I Heard Him Say to me:

My Holy Church!

I knew he was speaking pertaining to the H. on my right hand side. After a pause he said

The Harlot Church!

This he was speaking pertaining to the H. on my left hand side.

I began to weep uncontrollably in my dream. I knew in my heart that it was 3 AM in the morning. As I opened my eyes, (wide awake) tears were rolling down my face. It was **3:12** in the morning.

Let him that has an ear, hear what the Spirit is saying to His Holy church!

CHAPTER NINE
God's Heart Broken

God wants to share His wealth, abundance, power, and glory that He was willing to pay the ultimate price to bring about a creation that would love Him. They would love Him to such an extent that no matter how He blessed them, they would not rise up against Him. He could cause them to become one with Him and yet be totally submitted in every area of their existence. It would have to be a creation that had already been tempted, tested, and tried. It would contain those who had experienced the evil of selfishness and rejected it in order to love their Creator. Beloved, this is what it's all about. We choose to love God more than ourselves or the pleasures of this present time. Therefore we are esteemed worthy of all that God is, has, or ever will be. According to the Scriptures we will rule and reign with Christ forever. Simply because He first loved us. We rise up against the sinful nature that is in our flesh, which has penetrated our souls, following our beloved Savior and Shepherd wherever He may lead.

Sufferings of Christ

The suffering of Christ is still a great mystery to many of those in the church even. This suffering did not begin in the garden of Gethsemane. It literally began before the creation of all things. The Scriptures declared He was slain before the foundations of the world.

"And all that dwell upon the earth shall worship him, whose names are not written in the book of life of the Lamb slain from the foundation of the world" (Rev 13:8).

"But with the precious blood of Christ, as of a lamb without blemish and without spot: Who verily was foreordained before the foundation of the world, but was manifest in these last times for you" (1 Pet. 1:19-20).

From His birth to His resurrection Jesus Christ has suffered for you and me. In Isaiah chapter 53 it says He was a man of sorrows and acquainted with grief. It broke His heart to see the masses of humanity reject Him as their Messiah. For He knew that there was no other way than through Himself for men to be saved. We can only become partakers of the divine nature through the seed of Christ within the soil of our hearts.

It truly is all about Jesus. I would challenge every believer to buy a new Bible, and with a yellow highlighter, highlight every time it refers to Jesus in an intimate and personal way beginning in Matthew through the end of the book of Revelation. You would be amazed and shocked to discover that the Scriptures refer to Jesus approximately ten thousand times. That's ten thousand times in approximately 160 pages.

As we see Jesus moving toward His ultimate sacrifice, His personal suffering increased. The night He was betrayed by Judas, He sweat great drops of blood (see Luke 24:44). He declared that His soul was close to death because of His suffering. All of the sins of humanity were being poured into Him. He never committed sin, but Scripture says that He was made sin that we might be made to be partakers of His righteousness. All of His suffering—the stripes upon His back, the crown of thorns upon His head, His beard being ripped out of His face, the spitting mocking and bruising of His body, dragging that rugged cross up Golgotha's hill— was for our salvation. When they threw His body down upon the tree and nailed His feet and hands to it with spikes, Christ, God in the flesh, allowed Himself to be brutalized and violated for our salvation. Even the heavenly Father had to turn His back upon His own son. Can you imagine how it broke the Father's heart for Him to have to turn His back on His only begotten Son?

"And about the ninth hour Jesus cried with a loud voice, saying, Eli, Eli, lama sabachthani? that is to say, My God, my God, why hast thou forsaken me?" (Matt. 27:46).

How could any human being not love Him? But that was not the end of His suffering. Scripture declares His soul descended into hell. This is very important for us to understand. His Spirit did not descend into hell, but it returned to the Father from which it came.

"And when Jesus had cried with a loud voice, he said, Father, into thy hands I commend my spirit: and having said thus, he gave up the spirit" (Luke 23:46).

"He seeing this before spake of the resurrection of Christ, that his soul was not left in hell, neither his flesh did see corruption. This Jesus hath God raised up, whereof we all are witnesses" *(Acts 2:31-32).*

The reason why there is so much confusion in some of these areas of understanding is because we have not rightly discerned the Word of truth. Many years ago I discovered not to wrestle with the Word but simply to acknowledge, and believe, even if it contradicts everything I've ever been taught. I simply embrace the truth no matter where it leads. And then God gives me understanding within the context of those Scriptures. It is a wonderful and beautiful freedom. It is only when we allow the philosophy and indoctrination of naturally thinking men, which contradicts the teaching of God's Word, to influence our lives that we wrestle with the scriptures. This also gives the enemy of our soul, the devil, the right to blind our eyes from the truth.

The soul of Christ took the sins of humanity into the depths of hell to be left there forever. Jesus is able to help us because He knows the pains and sufferings of not only life but separation from the Father. He knows the torments of hell. Surely we can trust our eternal souls to such a loving Savior.

Tri-unity of Man

The Scriptures reveal that man is a three-part being. The three parts of man are composed of his soul, spirit, and body. There seems to be a lot of misunderstanding over man's three-part composition. Virtually, a book alone could be written on this particular subject. For us to truly comprehend what hell is all about we need to understand who and what man is. Really the Scriptures are quite informative and descriptive pertaining to this area. (Many times our indoctrination interferes with this revelation.)

When my wife and I attended Bible college, we were taught that we were a spirit, that we have a soul, and that we live in a physical body. If you diligently search the Scriptures I think you will discover that this is not the correct makeup of man's composition.

Man is a soul.

Over eleven hundred times within the Scriptures the Bible talks about man's soul. We only need to use a small portion of the Scriptures to reveal the truth about this divine mystery. Genesis declared that man became a living soul. The soul of man is also considered his heart—our thoughts, intents, and purposes, that which decides and determines our eternal destiny.

"And the LORD God formed man of the dust of the ground, and breathed into his nostrils the breath of life; and man became a living soul" (Gen. 2:7).

"And so it is written, The first man Adam was made a living soul; the last Adam was made a quickening spirit" (1 Cor. 15:45).

It is the soul of man that commits sin. It is also the soul of man that dies. The Spirit of the Lord in man did not die as many have been taught. When man committed sin in the garden, he was warned that he would die. It was the soul that God was warning him about. At that moment the human soul died to its responsiveness, sensitivity, and love for God. The heart and soul received the corruptible seed of Satan and became a lover of self and the flesh. The controlling and dominating aspect of the human soul came under the influence of corrupted flesh, where at one time it was under the influence of God's Spirit.

"The soul that sinneth, it shall die" (Ezek. 18:20a).

"And you hath he quickened, who were dead in trespasses and sins; Wherein in time past ye walked according to the course of this world, according to the prince of the power of the air, the spirit that now worketh in the children of disobedience: Among whom also we all had our conversation in times past in the lusts of our flesh, fulfilling the desires of the flesh and of the mind; and were by nature the children of wrath, even as others" (Eph. 2:1-3).

It is the soul of man that goes to hell and not the spirit. The unconverted souls of humanity are eternally separated from God and quarantined in hell.

It is the soul (the heart) of man that must be converted. It is in the soul that believers experience a new birth. The incorruptible seed of God's divine nature must be implanted into the soil of the soul of man. Our souls must be converted, transformed, renewed, and saved. Jesus came to save our souls.

"Brethren, if any of you do err from the truth, and one convert him; Let him know, that he which converteth the sinner from the error his way shall save a soul from death, and shall hide a multitude of sins" (James 5:19-20).

"Receiving the end of your faith, even the salvation of your souls" (1 Pet. 1:9).

Please keep in mind that when the Scriptures are talking about the human soul it is referring to the human heart.

"The heart is deceitful above all things, and desperately wicked: who can know it?" (Jer. 17:9).

"This is an evil among all things that are done under the sun, that there is one event unto all: yea, also the heart of the sons of men is full of evil, and madness is in their heart while they live, and after that they go to the dead" (Eccles. 9:3).

The human soul is one of God's most amazing creations. It bridges the gap of the spiritual and the natural. It literally straddles both dimensions. The human soul was created to house the very essence of God Himself. The Scriptures declare that we are His tabernacle. We are to be the dwelling place of God's presence. The demonic world wanted to sit upon God's throne. That's why they endeavor to possess our souls. In order to get a glimpse of the capacity of the human soul we just need to take a look at the example within the Scriptures. When Jesus cast the devils out of the man from the region of the Gadarenes, the demons declared that they were a legion. In that particular time a full strength of a legion of Roman soldiers was officially made up of 5,200 men. (18)

Could it possibly be that this man's soul was inhabited by six thousand devils? Yes, I believe he was. This reveals the capacity of the human soul, which was made to be inhabited by God's Spirit.

Man has a spirit.

The word spirit is used many times within the Bible. You have to study the context to see what it is referring to. It could be referring to angelic, demonic, the Holy Spirit, or the human spirit. It can also be referring to the attitude or the disposition of a person. A perfect example is when Scripture says that Joshua and Caleb had a different spirit about them.

"But my servant Caleb, because he had another spirit with him, and hath followed me fully, him will I bring into the land where into he went; and his seed shall possess it" (Num. 14:24).

"We having the same spirit of faith, according as it is written, I believed, and therefore have I spoken; we also believe, and therefore speak" (2 Cor. 4:13).

In the Garden of Eden, God breathed into man the breath of life. When the soul of man died in the garden, he did not lose the Spirit of God. The Spirit of God still resides in his flesh. Actually the Spirit of God is the life of the flesh. It is only when the Spirit leaves man that the flesh will die. The human spirit is similar to electricity in the sense that it provides the active energy of the human flesh. Of course it is much deeper than this simple statement.

"The burden of the word of the LORD for Israel, saith the LORD, which stretcheth forth the heavens, and layeth the foundation of the earth, and formeth the spirit of man within him" (Zech. 12:1).

"The Spirit of God hath made me, and the breath of the Almighty hath given me life" (Job 33:4).

The spirit within man is the conscience of his heart. It is to be the divine guidance system for his soul given by God. It is the "GPS of man's life." The spirit that God put within man's flesh never died. Men throughout the ages have either yielded or ignored the voice of His Spirit. As I stated there needs to be a whole book written on this particular subject. The description that I am giving here is really an oversimplification of the deep mysteries of the kingdom of God. Man is fearfully and wonderfully made.

"But there is a spirit in man: and the inspiration of the Almighty giveth them understanding" (Job 32:8).

"For what man knoweth the things of a man, save the spirit of man which is in him? even so the things of God knoweth no man, but the Spirit of God" (1 Cor. 2:11).

When a person dies outside of Christ the spirit returns to God from whence it came. But his soul goes to hell. The soul (heart) is who you really are. The human spirit is not re-created at the new birth. The spirit of man never died; it was his soul. Our souls need to be born again. Our souls need to be saved.

"Then shall the dust return to the earth as it was: and the spirit shall return unto God who gave it" (Eccles. 12:7).

"If he set his heart upon man, if he gather unto himself his spirit and his breath; All flesh shall perish together, and man shall turn again unto dust" (Job 34:14-15). [This is referring to his body!]

Man inhabits a body.

Yes, the human body is an amazing machine. But the simple truth is that it was not created through a process of evolution. It was created by the spirit that God breathed into it. And when you and I die, the human body will turn back to dust from whence it came. Then at the return of Christ those who are saved will receive a glorified body. But those who are damned will not receive an indestructible body till after the thousand-year reign of Christ. Then their souls with their re-created bodies will be cast into the lake of fire with the devil and his angels for all eternity.

"Thou hidest thy face, they are troubled: thou takest away their breath, they die, and return to their dust" (Ps. 104:29).

"And many of them that sleep in the dust of the earth shall awake, some to everlasting life, and some to shame and everlasting contempt" (Dan. 12: 2).

The conclusion of what we have just briefly studied is that you and I are a soul. We have a spirit that comes from God Almighty. And we are housed in a physical body. Christ died to save our souls. When a person dies loving Christ, his soul becomes one with the Spirit of God for eternity. It is like that of the seed of man, entering into the egg of the woman, thereby creating a human life. The new birth and the life of the believer is similar in that a son of God comes forth. We enter into an immortal eternal life. And our corrupted body will put on incorruption, and mortality will put on immortality.

CHAPTER TEN

Conclusion

I have shared with you from my heart some of the experiences that the Lord has allowed me to go through. I know that what I have shared could never capture to the fullest extent what took place in my journey to my time spent in heaven. But I pray that the Lord has used it to touch your life in some degree. The harvest is truly great, but the laborers are few. I hope this book would become a catalyst that God could use to bring about a supernatural, enabling encounter with Him. If there was ever a time the body of Christ needs to be active, it is now.

"No man that warreth entangleth himself with the affairs of this life; that he may please him who hath chosen him to be a soldier"(2Tim.2:4).

You see, God is not a respecter of persons. But every one of us has a different job, a different position, a unique place within the body. Do not believe or accept the lie that God does not have a specific purpose for your life. After God created the heavens and the earth, He put in to place a new law. God made it so that man became the gateway, channel, and avenue by which He would move, rule, and reign. There are an overwhelming amount of Scriptures that clearly proclaimed this a mazing truth. Hebrews chapter eleven reveals the names of twenty-two people God used to bring about His ultimate purpose and plan. The entire Bible is a declaration that it is now through man that God steps into the midst of humanity. God is looking and searching for men and women who will agree with His heart.

"And God blessed them, and God said unto them, Be fruitful, and multiply, and replenish the earth, and subdue it: and have dominion over the fish of the sea, and over the fowl of the air, and over every living thing that moveth upon the earth" (Gen. 1:28).

"For the prophecy came not in old time by the will of man: but holy men of God spake as they were moved by the Holy Ghost" (2 Pet. 1:21).

The heavenly Father stepped into this world through Jesus Christ to deliver, heal, save, and set men free. He was the physical embodiment of all that the heavenly Father is. He is the answer and solution to all of the world's problems.

"Neither is there salvation in any other: for there is none other name under heaven given among men, whereby we must be saved" (Acts 4:12).

Now it is our turn to be surrendered and submitted to the heavenly Father, His precious Son, and the Holy Ghost. We were made to be possessed, inhabited, filled, and under the influence of the Three in One. God has given to us the opportunity to be coworkers in the harvest field. Let us go forth in His mighty name. By His divine grace, power, authority, and His name may we go forth to set the multitudes free!

Note to Sinners and Backsliders

For those who possibly are not right with God, the story I have just shared with you truly happened to me. The Bible says that:

"By faith Noah, being warned of God of things not seen as yet, moved with fear, prepared an ark to the saving of his house; by the which he condemned the world, and became heir of the righteousness which is by faith" (Heb. 11:7).

God is moving in my heart with tremendous love and fear for you and for all of those who might not love God. I beg you and plead with you, in the name of Jesus Christ of Nazareth, to turn from your selfish, sinful, wicked ways and claim a new life in Jesus Christ. Or you will go to a burning hell. Once you have crossed the dark river of death, never more will you see a flower or green pastures or rolling oceans. Never will you again enjoy a glass of clear pure water or the simple pleasures of life. You will never again enjoy the sweet communion with those you love and know. But you will be lost forever in the endless ages of eternal darkness and fire.

Darkness and pain, torment and sorrow will be your eternal destiny. Shaking hands with a preacher will not save you. Putting your name on a church membership list will not do it. Giving money to a ministry or doing good deeds of any kind will not get you to heaven. We must repent of willful, known sin, and we must have a Godly sorrow for our actions. We must ask God, out of the depths of our hearts, to forgive us. And no matter how great our sin is, if we are sincere and no longer want to stay in our sins, God will deliver and forgive and accept us. Oh, sinner, be warned while there is yet time, and the eyes of the Savior still plead, and Jesus still beckons. Leave the broad and wide path of a selfish life, which leads to hell. And walk upon the straight and narrow way, which leads to heaven.

Remember how the demons cried out and asked Jesus whether He had come to torment them before their time? Are we so foolish as to not be moved by the realities of hell or to make light of them? Christianity consists of a new heart and a new life, dedicated and committed to not sinning. It is living for the glory of God. If your heart and life has not been changed by God, if you are still living in open rebellion and known disobedience to the Word and will of God, and you are not concerned about it, you have no right to assume you are going to heaven.

The devil and his demons will have the right to grab you by the hair, by your arms and legs, and pull you to hell with them. Sin is worse than hell because sin made it necessary for Jesus to create such a place called hell. It is the ultimate conclusion of a sinful life. Please, flee from sin! Flee from living for yourself. Flee from being self-pleasing, self-serving, self-loving, and self-centered. When you die, it will be too late to turn away from your sins. All opportunity to turn to God ends at death. Unless you turn from your selfishness and run to Jesus Christ and believe on Him who is our only hope, you will curse God eternally. And you will never die to the pains, agonies, terrors, horrors, and sorrows of hell. You will never experience the glory of heaven.

"Many will say to me in that day, Lord, Lord, have we not prophesied in thy name? and in thy name have cast out devils? and in thy name done many wonderful works? and then will I profess unto them, I never knew you: depart from me, ye that work iniquity" (Matt. 7:22).

I pray with all of my heart that this experience God allowed me to have will cause you to look to the loving Savior who poured out His lifeblood for you and who was nailed to the cross for your sins. He lovingly and longingly desires you to become one of His children. Won't you believe upon Him today? Call out to Him today. He will in no way cast out any who come to Him. Please, please turn from your wicked, evil, and self- centered ways. Love Him who first loved us. Let God give you a new heart and nature, a heart that loves, serves, and follows God. I hope to see you in heaven!

How to Live in the Miraculous!

This is a quick explanation of how to live and move in the realm of the miraculous. Seeing divine interventions of God is not something that just spontaneously happens because you have been born-again. There are certain biblical principles and truths that must be evident in your life. This is a very basic list of some of these truths and laws:

1.   You must give Jesus Christ your whole heart. You cannot be lackadaisical in this endeavour. Being lukewarm in your walk with God is repulsive to the Lord. He wants 100% commitment. Jesus gave His all, now it is our turn to give our all. He loved us 100%. Now we must love Him 100%.

My son, give me thine heart, and let thine eyes observe my ways

(Proverbs 23:26).

So then because thou art lukewarm, and neither cold nor hot, I will spew thee out of my mouth (Revelation 3:16).

2. **There must be a complete agreement with God's Word.** We must be in harmony with the Lord in our attitude, actions, thoughts, and deeds. Whatever the Word of God declares in the New Testament is what we wholeheartedly agree with.

Can two walk together, except they be agreed? (Amos 3:3).

For the eyes of the LORD run to and fro throughout the whole earth, to shew himself strong in the behalf of them whose heart is perfect toward him (2 Chronicles 16:9).

3. **Obey and do the Word from the heart, from the simplest to the most complicated request or command.** No matter what the Word says to do, do it! Here are some simple examples: Lift your hands in praise, in everything give thanks, forgive instantly, gather together with the saints, and give offerings to the Lord, and so on.

   I can of mine own self do nothing: as I hear, I judge: and my judgment is just; because I seek not mine own will, but the will of the Father which hath sent me (John 5:30).

4. **Make Jesus the highest priority of your life.** Everything you do, do not do it as unto men, but do it as unto God.

   If ye then be risen with Christ, seek those things which are above, where Christ sitteth on the right hand of God. Set your affection on things above, not on things on the earth (Colossians 3:1-2).

5. **Die to self! The old man says, "My will be done!"** The new man says, "God's will be done!"

   I am crucified with Christ: nevertheless I live; yet not I, but Christ liveth in me: and the life which I now live in the flesh

I live by the faith of the Son of God, who loved me, and gave himself for me (Galatians 2:20).

Now if we be dead with Christ, we believe that we shall also live with him (Romans 6:8).

6. **Repent the minute you get out of God's will**—no matter how minor, or small the sin may seem.

(Revelation 3:19).

As many as I love, I rebuke and chasten: be zealous therefore, and repent.

7. **Take one step at a time.** God will test you (not to do evil) to see if you will obey him. *Whatever He tells you to do: by His Word, by His Spirit, or within your conscience, do it.* He will never tell you to do something contrary to His nature or His Word!

For whosoever shall do the will of my Father which is in heaven, the same is my brother, and sister, and mother (Matthew 12:50).

Then went he down, and dipped himself seven times in Jordan, according to the saying of the man of God: and his flesh came again like unto the flesh of a little child, and he was clean (2 Kings 5:14).

ABOUT THE AUTHOR

Dr. Michael and Kathleen Yeager have served as pastors/apostles, missionaries, evangelists, broadcasters and authors for over four decades. They flow in the gifts of the Holy Spirit, teaching the Word of God with wonderful signs and miracles following in confirmation of God's Word. In 1983, they began Jesus is Lord Ministries International, where are the pastors to this date.

Websites Connected to Doc Yeager

www.docyeager.com

www.jilmi.org

www.wbntv.org

Books Written by Doc Yeager:

"Living in the Realm of the Miraculous #1"
"I need God Cause I'm Stupid"
"The Miracles of Smith Wigglesworth"
"How Faith Comes 28 WAYS"
"Horrors of Hell, Splendors of Heaven"
"The Coming Great Awakening"
"Sinners in The Hands of an Angry GOD",
(modernized)
"Brain Parasite Epidemic"
"My JOURNEY to HELL" - illustrated for teenagers
"Divine Revelation of Jesus Christ"
"My Daily Meditations"
"Holy Bible of JESUS CHRIST"
"War In The Heavenlies - (Chronicles of Micah)"
"Living in the Realm of the Miraculous #2"
"My Legal Rights to Witness"
"Why We (MUST) Gather! - 30 Biblical Reasons"
"My Incredible, Supernatural, Divine Experiences"
"Living in the Realm of the Miraculous #3"
"How GOD Leads & Guides! - 20 Ways"
"Weapons of Our Warfare"
"How You Can Be Healed"
"God Still Heals"
"God Still Provides"
"God Still Protects"
"Life Changing Quotes of Smith Wigglesworth"
"Hell Is For Real"
"Heaven Is For Real"
"How Faith Comes Work Book"
"How GOD Leads & Guides Work Book"

Made in United States
North Haven, CT
06 March 2023

33656919R00055